An Imprint of EWTECHNERD LLC
2040B South Church Street Ext
Spartanburg, SC 29306

Copyright 2023 by Jermaine Eric Whiteside EWTECHNERD supports copyright; copyright fuels creativity, encourages diverse voices, promotes free speech, and creates a vibrant culture. Thank you for buying an authorized edition of this book and complying with copyright laws by not reproducing, scanning, or distributing any part of it in any form without permission. You are supporting writers and allowing EWTECHNERD to continue to publish books for every reader.

LIBRARY OF CONGRESS CATALOGING IN PUBLICATION DATA
Names: Jermaine Eric Whiteside, Author
Title: EMPOWERING THE CARIBBEAN ISLANDS: The Role of Imports for Social Impact
Description, South Carolina
Identifiers:
CASE#

While the author has made every effort to provide accurate telephone numbers, internet addresses, and other contact information at the time of publication, EWTECHNERD LLC does not assume any responsibility for errors or changes that occur after publication. Further, the publisher has no control over and assumes no responsibility for the author, third-party websites, or their content.

AUTHOR

Jermaine Eric Whiteside is an experienced leader and passionate advocate for people. With a deep belief in the words of Jesus, "It is more blessed to give than to receive," Jermaine has dedicated his life to serving and empowering others through his various organizations and community involvement.

As the founder of Anointed Connect Church Inc, a recognized 501c3 church, Jermaine has worked tirelessly to serve and support his community. He is also the founder of Palmetto Leadership Institute, a recognized 501c3 charity organization, and the Co-Founder of Reinvest Carolina Inc, a recognized 501c3 charity for seniors and persons with disability housing. In addition to his work with charity organizations, Jermaine is also the Co-Founder of IAM Global Imports LTD.

Jermaine's leadership and dedication to good have also been recognized through his service on various boards. He currently serves on the Board of Directors for Veterans Services Commission Inc, Anointed Connect Church Inc, E-Vision Project Development Corporation, E-Visioneye Corporation, Active Expressions Art Academy, Reinvest

Carolina Inc, Reinvest America Corporation, and Truccit Corporation. He is also a member of the Board of Advisors for the UBBC Association.

In addition to his extensive experience and community involvement, Jermaine is a recent graduate of Walden University, where he earned his Master of Science in Information Management Systems. He also has executive education from top institutions such as Duke Fuqua School of Business, Harvard School of Law, Columbia Graduate School of Business, and MIT Executive Education. With this combination of education and experience, Jermaine is well-equipped to lead and serve in the importing and exporting industry for the Caribbean.

ACKNOWLEDGEMENT

"First and foremost, we would like to express our sincerest gratitude to God for His love and protection throughout the writing of this book. It is by His grace and guidance that this work has been made possible.

Psalm 18:2 says, "The Lord is my rock, my fortress, and my savior; in him I find protection. He is my shield, the strength of my life, and my stronghold." This book would not have been possible without the Lord's protection and guidance.

Proverbs 3:5-6 states, "Trust in the Lord with all your heart and lean not on your understanding; in all your ways submit to him, and he will make your paths straight." We have leaned on the Lord's understanding and submitted to His will in writing this book, and we are grateful for His guidance and direction.

Isaiah 41:10 says, "So do not fear, for I am with you; do not be dismayed, for I am your God. I will strengthen and help you and uphold you with my righteous right hand." We have felt the Lord's strength and help throughout the writing of this book, and we are grateful for His constant presence and support.

We also extend our gratitude to all those who have supported and encouraged us while writing this book. Your love, guidance, and help were invaluable, and we are deeply grateful for your presence in our lives."

FORWARD

I am honored to write the forward for this book, which delves into the critical issue of global imports for the public good in the Caribbean. The author has done an excellent job highlighting the many challenges the Caribbean islands

face, from economic vulnerability and trade imbalances to food security and health concerns.

One of the most striking aspects of this book is the emphasis on the role of faith-based organizations in addressing these challenges. As the Founder and Senior Pastor of Anointed Connect Church, Inc., I know firsthand the powerful impact these organizations can have on communities in need. Like many others in the Caribbean, our church has long been committed to serving our neighbors through various outreach programs, including food banks, health clinics, and education initiatives.

By partnering with government and private sector organizations, faith-based institutions can play an even more significant role in promoting economic development and improving the lives of Caribbean citizens. This book calls for all public and private organizations to work together to make a positive difference in the world.

The insights and recommendations presented in this book will be of great value to policymakers, business leaders, and community activists. I urge all readers to reflect on the critical issues raised in these pages and to consider how we can all play a part in creating a more prosperous and equitable future for the Caribbean.

As we embark on this journey, let us always remember to lean on the love and protection of God, as it says in Psalm 91:1-2 "He who dwells in the secret place of the Most High shall abide under the shadow of the Almighty. I will say of the Lord; He is my refuge and my fortress; my God, in Him I will trust."

In His Service,

Jermaine Eric Whiteside, Founder, Senior Pastor Anointed Connect Church, Inc.

Director, IAM Global Imports LTD

DEDICATION

"This book is first and foremost dedicated to God, who has provided the wisdom and guidance to address the issues faced by the Caribbean. It is a humble offering of gratitude and thanks for the blessings and provisions that have made this work possible. We dedicate this book to you with deep humility.

Additionally, this book is dedicated to the faith-based organizations and communities of the Caribbean, who tirelessly serve and empower their people. Their good work, dedication, and commitment to improving the lives of those around them are an inspiration and a shining example of the power of community.

This book will be a framework for governments of the Caribbean, who strive to improve the lives of their citizens and create a better future for all. It is a tribute to their hard work and determination, and their efforts to address the challenges faced by their people are admirable and make a real difference in the world."

EMPOWERING THE CARIBBEAN ISLANDS THE ROLE OF IMPORTS FOR SOCIAL IMPACT

1ST EDITION

PART OF THE ANOINTED THEOLOGICAL SEMINARY SERIES

INTEGRATION OF PUBLIC, PRIVATE, AND FAITH-BASED ORGANIZATIONS TO EMPOWER GOOD

ANOINTED THEOLOGICAL SEMINARY SERIES ATS INTERNAL 01152023-002

AUTHOR
JERMAINE ERIC WHITESIDE

TABLE OF CONTENTS

I. Introduction
   A. Background on the Caribbean region
   B. Purpose and scope of the book
   C. Overview of the critical issues and challenges

II. Economic Development
   A. The impact of imports on economic growth
   B. The role of imports in promoting small businesses and entrepreneurship
   C. Role of Faith-Based Organizations
   D. The relationship between imports and tourism development

III. Infrastructure and Public Services
   A. Imports and the development of transportation and communication infrastructure
   B. Imports and the provision of public services such as healthcare and education
   C. The role of imports in promoting digital inclusion and access to government services

IV. Energy and Environment
   A. Imports and the development of renewable energy in the Caribbean
   B. The relationship between imports and environmental protection
   C. The role of imports in addressing climate change and reducing dependence on fossil fuels

Trade and Investment

A. The impact of imports on trade and investment in the Caribbean

B. The role of imports in promoting regional integration and cooperation

C. The relationship between imports and foreign direct investment

INTRODUCTION

The Caribbean region, made up of more than 7,000 islands, is a diverse and dynamic part of the world with a rich cultural heritage and a complex history of colonialism, independence, and economic development. The Caribbean islands face several challenges, including limited resources, a fragile environment, and a small and vulnerable economy. Despite these challenges, the Caribbean has achieved economic growth and development, mainly using global imports.

This book will explore the role of global imports in promoting public goods in the Caribbean. It will examine the impact of imports on economic development, infrastructure, public services, energy and the environment, and trade and investment in the Caribbean. The book will also provide an overview of the critical issues and challenges facing the Caribbean and make recommendations for future action.

This book aims to provide a comprehensive and in-depth examination of the role of global imports in promoting public goods in the Caribbean. The book seeks to understand better the opportunities and challenges facing the Caribbean and identify ways in which global imports can be used to promote sustainable development and improve the lives of Caribbean people.

This book will interest policymakers, academics, business and faith-based leaders, and anyone interested in the Caribbean and the role of global trade in promoting the public good.

BACKGROUND OF THE CARIBBEAN REGION

The Caribbean region comprises more than 7,000 islands, islets, cays, and reefs in the Caribbean Sea, the Gulf of Mexico, and the Atlantic Ocean. The Caribbean islands are diverse and dynamic, with a rich cultural heritage and a complex history of colonialism, independence, and economic development.

The Caribbean islands are home to over 40 million people, with most of the population living in the larger islands, such as Cuba, Jamaica, and the Dominican Republic. The Caribbean islands have a small and vulnerable economy, with most countries depending on tourism, agriculture, and international trade as the primary sources of income.

The Caribbean islands have a fragile environment, with a high vulnerability to natural disasters such as hurricanes, earthquakes, and volcanic eruptions. Climate change is also a significant concern for the Caribbean, as rising sea levels and increased frequency of natural disasters can significantly impact the region's economy and environment.

Despite these challenges, the Caribbean has achieved some economic growth and development, mainly using global imports. The Caribbean countries have been able to access new technologies, products and services, and international markets through imports, which have helped to promote economic growth and development.

The Caribbean countries have also been able to improve the infrastructure and public services through global imports, which have helped to improve the quality of life of the Caribbean people. The Caribbean countries have also been able to use global implications to promote renewable energy development and reduce dependence on fossil fuels.

Overall, the Caribbean region is a complex and diverse area that faces several challenges but also has many opportunities for development and growth. Global imports can play an important role in promoting public good in the Caribbean and helping to improve the lives of the Caribbean people.

PURPOSE AND SCOPE

This book aims to analyze and explore the potential role of imports and exports in promoting economic development and public good in the Caribbean Islands. The scope of this book will include an examination of the trade imbalances, food security, health concerns, and infrastructure and public services in the Caribbean. It will also explore the potential of utilizing faith-based organizations as distribution locations and the relationship between imports and tourism development. This book will also explore the benefits of digital inclusion and access to technology for small businesses in the Caribbean and the role of imports in promoting small businesses and entrepreneurship.

Furthermore, this book will also provide recommendations for future action and strategies for the integration of public, private, and faith-based organizations for importing and exporting goods for the empowerment of the public in areas such as food security, education, housing, public safety, renewable energy, and technology innovation. This book aims to create economic growth models for Caribbean governments and restore faith-based structures.

OVERALL KEY ISSUES AND CHALLENGES

The Caribbean region highly depends on imports of various goods, including food, medicine, and other essential items. However, this dependence on global imports can lead to several challenges and issues that must be addressed. These include:

Economic vulnerability: The Caribbean economies are heavily dependent on tourism and foreign investment, making them vulnerable to global economic downturns. This vulnerability is exacerbated by the region's dependence on imported goods, which can become more expensive during economic recessions.

Trade imbalances: The Caribbean countries are generally net importers, meaning they import more goods than they export. This can lead to trade imbalances and a need for foreign currency, making it difficult for these countries to pay for imported goods.

Food security: Many Caribbean countries import a significant portion of their food, leaving them vulnerable to food shortages and price hikes. This is particularly problematic for small island nations, where food imports can make up a large percentage of the overall import bill.

Environmental impacts: Importing goods from other countries can have negative ecological impacts, such as increased carbon emissions from transportation and deforestation.

Lack of local production: Over-reliance on imports can lead to a lack of local production and can reduce the resilience of a local economy

Health concerns: Importing food and medicine can sometimes lead to public health concerns, as there is a risk that these products may not meet the same safety and quality standards as those produced locally.

Overall, the Caribbean region faces several challenges related to its dependence on global imports. Addressing these issues will require a combination of trade policy reform, investment in local production, and efforts to improve food and medicine safety.

ECONOMIC VULNERABILITY

The Caribbean islands are highly vulnerable to global economic downturns due to their heavy dependence on tourism and foreign investment. Tourism is a significant source of income for many Caribbean countries, and a downturn in the global economy can lead to a decrease in the number of tourists visiting the region. This, in turn, can lead to a reduction in foreign currency and a decrease in demand for imported goods, making it difficult for Caribbean countries to pay for the goods they need.

Furthermore, the Caribbean islands also depend on foreign investment, which can be affected by the global economic climate. A decrease in foreign investment can reduce job opportunities and economic growth, making it difficult for Caribbean countries to develop their economies and reduce their dependence on imported goods.

Additionally, the Caribbean region is exposed to external economic shocks due to its heavy reliance on imports, which can become more expensive during economic downturns. This can lead to inflation and a decrease in the standard of living for the population.

In summary, the Caribbean islands are highly vulnerable to global economic downturns due to their heavy dependence

on tourism and foreign investment. This vulnerability is further exacerbated by their reliance on imported goods, which can become more expensive during economic recessions and lead to inflation and a decreased standard of living. To address this issue, Caribbean countries will need to diversify their economies and find ways to reduce their dependence on imported goods.

TRADE IMBALANCES

The Caribbean islands generally have trade imbalances, meaning they import more goods than they export. This can lead to a lack of foreign currency, making it difficult for these countries to pay for imported goods.

One of the leading causes of trade imbalances in the Caribbean is the region's heavy dependence on imported goods. Many Caribbean countries import a significant portion of their food and other essential items, leaving them vulnerable to food shortages and price hikes. Many Caribbean countries also import raw materials for their manufacturing industries, which can be more expensive than producing them locally.

Another cause of trade imbalances in the Caribbean is the need for more diversification in the export sector. Many Caribbean countries rely heavily on key exports, such as tourism and a few agricultural products, which can make them vulnerable to fluctuations in demand for these products.

Trade barriers and lack of access to foreign markets can also contribute to trade imbalances in the Caribbean. Many Caribbean countries have small domestic markets, which makes it difficult for them to export their goods.

In conclusion, trade imbalances in the Caribbean are caused by a combination of factors, including the region's heavy dependence on imported goods, lack of diversification in the export sector, trade barriers, and lack of access to foreign markets. Addressing these imbalances will require a combination of trade policy reform, local production investment, and export sector diversification.

FOOD SECURITY

Food security is a significant concern for many Caribbean islands, as they heavily depend on imports for their food supply. This dependence on imported food can make these countries vulnerable to food shortages and price hikes.

One of the leading causes of food insecurity in the Caribbean is the lack of local food production. Many Caribbean countries have limited arable land and a small domestic market, making it difficult to produce enough food to meet their needs. Additionally, the Caribbean islands are often affected by natural disasters such as hurricanes, which can damage crops and infrastructure, further reducing their ability to produce food.

Another cause of food insecurity in the Caribbean is the high cost of imported food. Many Caribbean countries have high import tariffs and need access to foreign markets, making imported food more expensive than locally produced food. Additionally, the Caribbean countries are exposed to price volatility of food commodities in the international market. This can lead to food price inflation, making it more difficult for low-income households to afford food.

In conclusion, food security is a significant concern for many Caribbean islands due to their heavy dependence on imports for their food supply. This dependence is caused by a combination of factors, including lack of local food production, high cost of imported food, price volatility of

food commodities in the international market, and vulnerability to natural disasters. To address this issue, Caribbean countries will need to invest in local food production and storage infrastructure and develop policies that can help to increase access to affordable food.

HEALTH CONCERNS

Importing goods, particularly food and medicine, can sometimes lead to public health concerns in the Caribbean islands. One of the main concerns is that imported goods may need to meet the same safety and quality standards as those produced locally.

One of the leading causes of health concerns related to imports is the lack of proper regulations and inspection of imported goods. Many Caribbean countries need more resources and capacity to properly inspect and regulate imported goods, which can increase the risk of unsafe or contaminated products entering the country.

Another concern is that some imported goods may need to meet the nutritional requirements of the local population. For example, Caribbean countries may import processed foods high in sugar and sodium, which can contribute to health problems such as obesity and diabetes.

The lack of access to affordable and quality medicine is also a significant concern in the Caribbean islands. Many Caribbean countries have limited domestic production of pharmaceuticals and high import tariffs, making it difficult to access the necessary treatment for the population.

Health concerns about importing in Caribbean islands include the lack of proper regulations and inspection of imported goods. The risk of unsafe or contaminated products entering the country, the lack of access to affordable and quality medicine, and the possibility that imported goods may not meet the nutritional requirements of the local population. Caribbean countries must invest in regulations and inspection systems and work to increase access to affordable and quality medicine.

ECONOMIC DEVELOPMENT

Importing goods for low-density populations in the Caribbean can positively and negatively impact economic development.

On the one hand, importing goods can help meet the population's basic needs, such as food and medicine, improving the standard of living. Additionally, importing goods can provide access to a broader range of products and services, increasing consumer choice and enhancing economic opportunities.

On the other hand, importing goods can also negatively impact economic development. More reliance on imports can lead to a lack of local production and reduce a local economy's resilience. This can lead to a lack of jobs and economic opportunities, negatively impacting the population and hindering economic development. Additionally, importing goods can also increase the trade deficit and lead to a lack of foreign currency, making it difficult for the country to pay for imports in the future.

Furthermore, for low-density populations in the Caribbean, the high cost of transportation, combined with the small domestic markets, can make it difficult for them to compete with larger international suppliers, leading to a lack of local production.

Overall, the impact of importing goods on economic development for low-density populations in the Caribbean is complex and multifaceted. While imports can provide access to basic needs and a more comprehensive range of products and services, they can also lead to a lack of local production and economic opportunities. Caribbean countries must reduce their dependence on imported goods and develop policies promoting local production and economic development.

ROLE OF SMALL BUSINESSES AND ENTREPRENEURS

Imports can be essential in promoting small businesses and entrepreneurship in the Caribbean islands.

Firstly, imports can provide small businesses access to a broader range of products and services, increasing consumer choice and improving economic opportunities. Small companies can also import goods at lower prices and then sell them at a profit, which can help them to grow and create jobs.

Secondly, imports can also help small businesses to diversify their product offerings and reduce their dependence on a few essential products or services. This can help to make their businesses more resilient to fluctuations in demand and can help to improve their long-term viability.

The Caribbean islands can also use imports to access new markets and customers. By importing goods and services from other countries, small businesses can tap into new customer bases and increase their revenue.

Furthermore, Imports can also help small businesses and entrepreneurs to improve their competitiveness by providing access to new technologies and management practices. This can help them improve the quality of their products and services, leading to increased sales and improved profitability.

In conclusion, imports can promote small businesses and entrepreneurship in the Caribbean islands. Implications can provide small businesses access to a broader range of products and services, diversify their product offerings, access new markets and customers, and improve competitiveness. To fully benefit from imports, Caribbean countries must develop policies and programs that support small businesses and entrepreneurship, such as providing access to financing, training, and other resources.

ROLE OF FAITH-BASED ORGANIZATIONS

Faith-based organizations can be important in utilizing imports as distribution locations in Caribbean islands.

Faith-based organizations often have strong connections to their communities and are well-respected, making them effective distribution locations for imported goods. They can help to increase access to goods and services, particularly in underserved or remote areas where traditional distribution channels may be limited.

Faith-based organizations can also reduce the costs associated with importing goods by acting as distribution locations. By using these organizations, companies and organizations can avoid the need to build and maintain their distribution centers and can instead rely on existing infrastructure.

Additionally, faith-based organizations can also help to improve the transparency and accountability of the import process. They can act as an intermediary between the importers and the local communities, ensuring that the goods are distributed fairly and equitably.

Furthermore, faith-based organizations can also act as a bridge between the local communities and the government, providing information and support for policies and programs that will help address the population's needs.

In conclusion, faith-based organizations can be crucial in utilizing imports as distribution locations in Caribbean islands. They can help to increase access to goods and services, reduce the costs associated with importing goods, improve the transparency and accountability of the import process, and act as a bridge between the local communities and the government. To fully benefit from this role, Caribbean countries must develop policies and programs that support faith-based organizations and build partnerships between them and the private sector and government.

RELATIONSHIP BETWEEN IMPORTS AND TOURISM DEVELOPMENT

The relationship between imports and tourism development in Caribbean islands is complex and multifaceted.

On the one hand, imports can play a positive role in tourism development by providing access to a wide range of goods and services necessary for the tourism industry to operate. These include food and beverage products, hotel and resort supplies, transportation equipment, and other goods and services.

Furthermore, imports can also help to improve the quality of tourism-related products and services by providing access to new technologies and management practices. This can attract more tourists to the Caribbean islands and improve the overall competitiveness of the tourism industry.

On the other hand, imports can also negatively impact tourism development in the Caribbean islands. For example, the high cost of imported goods and services can make it difficult for small, locally owned businesses to compete with larger, international companies. This can lead to a lack of economic opportunities for local communities and can negatively impact the overall development of the tourism industry.

Additionally, the Caribbean islands are exposed to price volatility of tourism-related commodities in the international market. This can lead to increased costs for tourism operators, which can lead to higher prices for tourists, negatively impacting the competitiveness of the Caribbean tourism industry.

In conclusion, the relationship between imports and tourism development in Caribbean islands is complex and multifaceted. Imports can play a positive role by providing access to goods and services necessary for the tourism industry. Imports improve the quality of tourism-related products and services and can have negative impacts: the difficulty for small, locally owned businesses to compete increasing costs for tourism operators exposing them to price volatility of tourism-related commodities in the international market

To fully benefit from imports, Caribbean countries will need to develop policies and programs that balance the need for imported goods and services with the need to support local businesses and communities and address the negative impacts of imports on the tourism industry.

INFRASTRUCTURE AND PUBLIC SERVICES

Global imports for the public good can positively and negatively impact infrastructure and public services in the Caribbean islands.

On the positive side, imports can provide access to goods and services necessary for maintaining and improving infrastructure and public services. For example, imports can provide access to building materials, medical equipment, and other goods needed to construct new infrastructure and maintain existing infrastructure.

Additionally, imports can provide access to advanced technologies and management practices, which can help to improve the quality and efficiency of public services.

However, on the negative side, imports can also negatively impact infrastructure and public services in the Caribbean islands. For example, the high cost of imported goods and services can make it difficult for the government to afford to maintain and improve infrastructure and public services. Additionally, the dependence on imports can lead to a lack of local production and reduce the local economy's resilience. This can lead to a lack of jobs and economic opportunities, negatively impacting the population and hindering economic development.

Furthermore, the Caribbean islands are also exposed to price volatility of imported goods and services in the international market. This can lead to increased costs for the government, leading to higher costs for the population, which can negatively impact the quality of public services. In conclusion, global imports for public goods can positively and negatively impact the Caribbean islands' infrastructure and public services. Imports can provide access to necessary goods and services for maintaining and improving infrastructure and public services. However, it also can make it difficult for the government to maintain and improve infrastructure and public services, leading to a lack of local production and exposing the price volatility of imported goods and services in the international market. To fully benefit from imports, Caribbean countries will need to develop policies and programs that balance the need for imported goods and services with the need to support local businesses and communities and address the negative impacts of imports on infrastructure and public services.

DEVELOPMENT OF TRANSPORTATION AND COMMUNICATION INFRASTRUCTURE

Imports for public goods can significantly impact the development of transportation and communication infrastructure in Caribbean islands.

On the positive side, imports can provide access to goods and services necessary for constructing and maintaining transportation and communication infrastructure. This includes vehicles, equipment, and technology, such as vehicles, construction equipment, and communication technologies. These goods and services can help improve the quality and efficiency of transportation and communication infrastructure and make it easier for people to move around the islands and stay connected.

Additionally, imports can help improve the quality of transportation and communication infrastructure by providing access to new technologies and management practices. This can help improve the speed, reliability, and safety of transportation and communication systems, improving the overall quality of life for the population.

However, on the negative side, imports can also negatively impact transportation and communication infrastructure in the Caribbean islands. For example, the high cost of imported goods and services can make it difficult for the government to afford to maintain and improve transportation and communication infrastructure. Additionally, the dependence on imports can also lead to a lack of local production and can reduce the local economy's resilience. This can lead to a lack of jobs and economic opportunities, negatively impacting the population and hindering economic development.

Furthermore, the Caribbean islands are also exposed to price volatility of imported goods and services in the international market. This can lead to increased costs for the government, which can lead to higher costs for the population, negatively impacting the quality of transportation and communication infrastructure.

In conclusion, imports for the public good can significantly impact the development of transportation and communication infrastructure in Caribbean islands. Imports can provide access to goods and services that are necessary for the construction and maintenance of transportation and communication infrastructure and provide access to new technologies and management practices. However, it also can make it difficult for the government to afford to maintain and improve transportation and communication infrastructure, lead to a lack of local production, and expose to price volatility of imported goods and services in the international market. To fully benefit from imports, Caribbean countries will need to develop policies and programs that balance the need for imported goods and services with the need to support local businesses and communities and address the negative impacts of imports on transportation and communication infrastructure.

IMPORTS AND THE PROVISION OF PUBLIC SERVICES SUCH AS HEALTHCARE AND EDUCATION

Imports for public goods can significantly impact public services such as healthcare and education in Caribbean islands.

On the positive side, imports can provide access to goods and services necessary to provide healthcare and education services. This includes medical equipment, pharmaceuticals, and educational materials. These goods and services can help to improve the quality and accessibility of healthcare and education services and can make it easier for people to access these services.

Additionally, imports can help improve the quality of healthcare and education services by providing access to new technologies and management practices. This can help improve the efficiency and effectiveness of healthcare and education systems, improving the overall quality of life for the population.

However, on the negative side, imports can also negatively impact the provision of public services such as healthcare and education in Caribbean islands. For example, the high cost of imported goods and services can make it difficult for the government to afford to provide healthcare and education services. Additionally, the dependence on imports can lead to a lack of local production and reduce the local economy's resilience. This can lead to a lack of jobs and economic opportunities, negatively impacting the population and hindering economic development.

Furthermore, the Caribbean islands are also exposed to price volatility of imported goods and services in the international market. This can lead to increased costs for the government, which can lead to higher costs for the population, negatively impacting the quality of healthcare and education services. In conclusion, imports for public goods can significantly impact the provision of public services such as healthcare and education in Caribbean islands.

THE ROLE OF IMPORTS IN PROMOTING DIGITAL INCLUSION AND ACCESS TO GOVERNMENT SERVICES

Imports for the public good can be essential in promoting digital inclusion and access to government services in Caribbean islands.

Firstly, imports can provide access to technological goods and services necessary for digital inclusion. This includes computers, smartphones, and internet access, which can help to bridge the digital divide and increase access to online services and information.

Secondly, imports can also help to improve the quality and accessibility of government services by providing access to new technologies and management practices. This can include e-government platforms, digital ID systems, and other digital tools that can help improve government services' efficiency and effectiveness.

Additionally, imports can also help to increase the digital literacy and skills of the population, making it easier for people to access government services and benefit from digital technologies.

Furthermore, Imports can also help improve the government's transparency and accountability by providing access to new technologies that can increase the transparency and openness of government information and decision-making processes.

In conclusion, imports for the public good can play an essential role in promoting digital inclusion and access to government services in Caribbean islands. Imports can provide access to technology goods and services, improve the quality and accessibility of government services, increase the population's digital literacy and skills, and improve the government's transparency and accountability. To fully benefit from imports, Caribbean countries must develop policies and programs that support digital inclusion and access to government services and build partnerships between the government, private sector, and civil society.

Digital inclusion and technology access can significantly benefit developing small businesses in the Caribbean islands.

Firstly, digital inclusion and access to technology can help small businesses to increase their reach and access new markets. This can include access to e-commerce platforms, digital marketing tools, and other online tools that can help small businesses connect with customers domestically and internationally.

Secondly, digital inclusion and access to technology can also help small businesses to improve their efficiency and productivity. This can include access to digital tools such as accounting software, project management tools, and other digital tools that can help small businesses to streamline their operations and improve their overall performance.

Additionally, digital inclusion and access to technology can also help small businesses to improve the quality of their products and services by providing access to new technologies and management practices. This can include access to technologies such as 3D printing, artificial intelligence, and other digital tools that can help small businesses to create new products and services and improve the quality of their existing offerings.

Furthermore, digital inclusion and access to technology can also help improve small businesses' transparency and accountability by providing access to new technologies that can increase the transparency and openness of their information and decision-making processes.

In conclusion, digital inclusion and technology access can significantly benefit developing small businesses in the Caribbean islands. It can help small businesses to increase their reach and access new markets, improve their efficiency and productivity, improve the quality of their products and

services, and enhance the transparency and accountability of their operations. To fully benefit from digital inclusion and access to technology, Caribbean countries must develop policies and programs that support digital inclusion and technology and build partnerships between small businesses and government, the private sector, and civil society.

ENERGY AND ENVIRONMENT

The Caribbean region faces several energy and environmental challenges related to importing fossil fuels to meet its energy needs. These include:

High costs: The Caribbean countries rely heavily on imported fossil fuels, which can be costly and strain their economies.

Energy security: The Caribbean countries are vulnerable to disruptions in the supply of fossil fuels due to factors such as natural disasters and political instability.

Environmental impacts: Burning fossil fuels contributes to climate change and air pollution, which can negatively impact the environment and human health.

Limited access to electricity: Many Caribbean countries have limited access to electricity, particularly in rural and remote areas.

Limited resources: Caribbean countries have small economies and often need more help and capacity to develop renewable energy independently.

Limited infrastructure: Caribbean countries also need more infrastructure to support the integration of renewable energy in the grid.

Balancing economic, social, and environmental factors: Caribbean countries need to balance economic, social, and environmental factors when developing renewable energy and importing technology, expertise, and equipment for renewable energy.

Lack of technical expertise. Caribbean countries have a low-density technical workforce, and expertise in developing and maintaining renewable energy systems requires importing expertise from other countries.

Caribbean countries need to take a holistic approach that includes the development of renewable energy, energy efficiency, and energy conservation measures, as well as importing technology, expertise, and equipment for renewable energy. This will help them reduce dependence on fossil fuels, improve energy security, boost economic growth and create jobs, and improve access to electricity for all sustainably.

IMPORTS AND THE DEVELOPMENT OF RENEWABLE ENERGY IN THE CARIBBEAN

Imports and the development of renewable energy in the Caribbean

The Caribbean region relies heavily on imported fossil fuels to meet its energy needs. However, these imports' increasing costs and environmental impacts have led to a growing interest in renewable energy as an alternative.

One of the significant benefits of renewable energy for the Caribbean is that it can reduce dependence on imported fossil fuels. This not only reduces costs for Caribbean countries but also improves energy security and reduces the region's greenhouse gas emissions.

Furthermore, the Caribbean is particularly well-suited for developing renewable energy due to its abundant solar, wind, and hydro resources. For example, many Caribbean islands receive high levels of solar radiation, making solar power an up-and-coming option.

Renewable energy development in the Caribbean can also create jobs and boost economic growth. In addition, it can improve access to electricity in rural and remote areas, which is a challenge in many Caribbean countries.

However, the development of renewable energy in the Caribbean has its challenges. The Caribbean countries are small economies and often need more resources and capacity to develop renewable energy independently. Therefore, the import of technology and expertise is required to support renewable energy development. The Caribbean countries also need to work on their infrastructures to support the integration of renewable energy in the grid.

In conclusion, imports of technology, expertise, and equipment for renewable energy can play a crucial role in developing renewable energy in the Caribbean. It can help Caribbean countries reduce dependence on fossil fuels, improve energy security, boost economic growth, create jobs, and improve access to electricity for all. However, it needs to be done sustainably, considering the economic, social, and environmental factors.

THE RELATIONSHIP BETWEEN IMPORTS AND ENVIRONMENTAL PROTECTION

The relationship between imports and environmental protection in Caribbean Islands is complex and multifaceted. On the one hand, imports can play a crucial role in helping Caribbean islands reduce their dependence on fossil fuels and develop renewable energy sources, which can have positive environmental impacts. However, on the other hand, imports can also contribute to ecological degradation if they are not managed and regulated effectively.

Imports of technology, expertise, and equipment for renewable energy can play a crucial role in developing renewable energy in the Caribbean. As mentioned earlier, Caribbean countries are small economies and often need more resources and capacity to develop renewable energy independently. Therefore, imports of technology and expertise are required to support renewable energy development. This can help Caribbean countries reduce dependence on fossil fuels, improve energy security, boost economic growth, and create jobs, and improve access to electricity for all in a sustainable way.

However, imports of goods and services can also contribute to environmental degradation if they are not managed and regulated effectively. For example, importing goods that are not produced in an environmentally sustainable way can contribute to deforestation, air pollution, and other environmental problems. Imports of goods that are not recycled or disposed of properly can also contribute to environmental degradation.

Caribbean countries must adopt sustainable import policies focusing on the environmental performance of imported goods and services. This could include policies that promote environmentally friendly technologies and products, encourage the use of recycled materials, and adopt environmentally friendly production processes.

In conclusion, imports can play a crucial role in developing renewable energy in the Caribbean and protecting the environment. However, Caribbean countries must adopt sustainable import policies that focus on the environmental performance of imported goods and services to mitigate the negative impacts of imports on the environment.

THE ROLE OF IMPORTS IN ADDRESSING CLIMATE CHANGE AND REDUCING DEPENDENCE ON FOSSIL FUELS

The Caribbean Islands are particularly vulnerable to the impacts of climate change, such as sea level rise, increased frequency and intensity of hurricanes and storms, and changes in precipitation patterns. Therefore, addressing climate change and reducing dependence on fossil fuels is vital for the Caribbean Islands.

Imports of technology, expertise, and equipment for renewable energy can play a crucial role in addressing climate change and reducing dependence on fossil fuels in the Caribbean. The Caribbean is particularly well-suited for developing renewable energy due to its abundant solar, wind, and hydro resources. Renewable energy development in the Caribbean can reduce dependence on imported fossil fuels, improve energy security, reduce greenhouse gas emissions, create jobs, and boost economic growth.

Furthermore, the Caribbean countries are small economies and often need more resources and capacity to develop renewable energy independently. Therefore, imports of technology and expertise are required to support renewable energy development. This includes importing solar panels, wind turbines, and hydroelectric equipment and the expertise to install and maintain them.

However, it is essential to note that renewable energy development in the Caribbean should be done sustainably, considering the economic, social, and environmental factors. The Caribbean countries also need to work on their infrastructures to support the integration of renewable energy in the grid, which may involve additional imports.

In conclusion, imports of technology, expertise, and equipment for renewable energy can play a crucial role in addressing climate change and reducing dependence on fossil fuels in the Caribbean. This can help Caribbean countries reduce dependence on fossil fuels, improve energy security, boost economic growth, create jobs, and reduce greenhouse gas emissions. However, renewable energy development must be done sustainably, considering the economic, social, and environmental factors.

TRADE AND INVESTMENT

Trade and investment are crucial for the Caribbean Islands to meet their energy needs and reduce dependence on fossil fuels. The Caribbean region relies heavily on imported fossil fuels to meet its energy needs, which can be costly and strain its economies. However, these imports' increasing costs and environmental impacts have led to a growing interest in renewable energy as an alternative.

Imports of technology, expertise, and equipment for renewable energy can play a crucial role in developing renewable energy in the Caribbean. The Caribbean is particularly well-suited for developing renewable energy due to its abundant solar, wind, and hydro resources. Renewable energy development in the Caribbean can reduce dependence on imported fossil fuels, improve energy security, reduce greenhouse gas emissions, create jobs, and boost economic growth.

The Caribbean countries are small economies and often need more resources and capacity to develop renewable energy independently. Therefore, imports of technology and expertise are required to support renewable energy development. This includes importing solar panels, wind turbines, and hydroelectric equipment and the expertise to install and maintain them.

Renewable energy development in the Caribbean can also create jobs and boost economic growth. In addition, it can improve access to electricity in rural and remote areas, which is a challenge in many Caribbean countries.

Moreover, trade and investment can also play a vital role in the Caribbean's transition to renewable energy by attracting foreign investment in renewable energy projects and creating new markets for Caribbean-produced renewable energy. This can finance the development of renewable energy and promote economic growth.

However, it is essential to note that renewable energy development in the Caribbean should be done sustainably, considering the economic, social, and environmental factors. The Caribbean countries also need to work on their infrastructures to support the integration of renewable energy in the grid, which may involve additional imports.

In conclusion, imports of technology, expertise, and equipment for renewable energy can play a crucial role in addressing climate change, reducing dependence on fossil fuels, and promoting economic growth in the Caribbean. However, renewable energy development must be done sustainably, considering the economic, social, and environmental factors. Trade and investment can also play a vital role in the Caribbean's transition to renewable energy by attracting foreign investment in renewable energy projects and creating new markets for Caribbean-produced renewable energy.

THE IMPACT OF IMPORTS ON TRADE AND INVESTMENT IN THE CARIBBEAN

The impact of importing for the public good on trade and investment in the Caribbean is complex and multifaceted. On the one hand, importing technology, expertise, and equipment for renewable energy can promote trade and investment by creating new markets for Caribbean-produced renewable energy and attracting foreign investment in renewable energy projects. On the other hand, trade and investment policies that need to be well-designed or implemented can negatively impact the Caribbean's ability to import for the public good.

In terms of trade, importing technology, expertise, and equipment for renewable energy can create new markets for Caribbean-produced renewable energy and promote economic growth. For example, if Caribbean countries import solar panels and wind turbines, they can then start producing and exporting renewable energy to other countries. This can help to create jobs and boost economic growth in the Caribbean.

In terms of investment, imports of technology, expertise, and equipment for renewable energy can also attract foreign investment in renewable energy projects. This can help finance renewable energy development and promote economic growth. Additionally, if the Caribbean countries can demonstrate their ability to develop and maintain renewable energy systems, it can attract more foreign investment in the Caribbean.

However, trade and investment policies that are not well-designed or implemented can have negative impacts on the Caribbean's ability to import for the public good. For example, suppose trade policies are not designed to promote environmentally friendly technologies and products. In that case, importing goods that are not produced in an environmentally sustainable way can contribute to environmental degradation. Similarly, if investment policies do not focus on the ecological performance of imported goods and services, they can contribute to environmental degradation.

In conclusion, importing technology, expertise, and equipment for renewable energy can positively impact trade and investment in the Caribbean by creating new markets for Caribbean-produced renewable energy and attracting foreign investment in renewable energy projects. However, it is essential that trade and investment policies are well-designed and implemented to promote environmentally friendly technologies and products and focus on the environmental performance of imported goods and services to mitigate the negative impacts of imports on the environment.

THE ROLE OF IMPORTS IN PROMOTING REGIONAL INTEGRATION AND COOPERATION

The Caribbean Islands are a diverse group of countries with unique energy needs and resources. However, regional integration and cooperation can play a crucial role in addressing these challenges and promoting renewable energy development in the Caribbean.

Imports of technology, expertise, and equipment for renewable energy can play a crucial role in promoting regional integration and cooperation in the Caribbean. By sharing knowledge and resources, Caribbean countries can collaborate to develop renewable energy projects and reduce dependence on fossil fuels. For example, one country might have abundant wind resources while another has abundant hydro resources. By working together, these countries can develop and export renewable energy to other countries and improve energy security.

Regional integration and cooperation can also help Caribbean countries overcome the challenges of limited resources and infrastructure. By pooling resources and working together, Caribbean countries can develop and implement renewable energy projects that are impossible on their own. This can also help to attract foreign investment in renewable energy projects, create jobs, and boost economic growth.

Furthermore, regional integration and cooperation can also help to improve access to electricity in rural and remote areas, which is a challenge in many Caribbean countries. By working together, Caribbean countries can develop and implement renewable energy projects that provide electricity to rural and remote areas that would not be possible on their own.

In conclusion, imports of technology, expertise, and equipment for renewable energy can play a crucial role in promoting regional integration and cooperation in the Caribbean. By sharing knowledge and resources, Caribbean countries can collaborate to develop renewable energy projects, reduce dependence on fossil fuels, and improve energy security. Furthermore, regional integration and cooperation can help Caribbean countries overcome the challenges of limited resources and infrastructure, improve access to electricity in rural and remote areas, and boost economic growth.

THE RELATIONSHIP BETWEEN IMPORTS AND FOREIGN DIRECT INVESTMENT

The relationship between imports for public goods and foreign direct investment (FDI) in Caribbean Islands is complex and multifaceted. On the one hand, imports of technology, expertise, and equipment for renewable energy can attract foreign direct investment in renewable energy projects, which can help to finance the development of renewable energy and promote economic growth. On the other hand, foreign direct investment can also be used to import goods and services that are not produced in an environmentally sustainable way, which can negatively impact the environment.

Imports of technology, expertise, and equipment for renewable energy can attract foreign direct investment in renewable energy projects in the Caribbean. For example, if Caribbean countries import solar panels and wind turbines, they can then start producing and exporting renewable energy to other countries. This can help to create jobs and boost economic growth in the Caribbean. Furthermore, if the Caribbean countries can demonstrate their ability to develop and maintain renewable energy systems, it can attract more foreign investment in the Caribbean.

Additionally, foreign direct investment can also be used to import goods and services that are not produced in an environmentally sustainable way, which can negatively impact the environment. For example, if a foreign company investing in the Caribbean is not using environmentally friendly technologies and products, it can contribute to environmental degradation.

To mitigate these negative impacts of foreign direct investment on the environment, Caribbean countries need to adopt sustainable trade and investment policies focusing on the environmental performance of imported goods and services. This could include policies that promote environmentally friendly technologies and products, encourage the use of recycled materials, and adopt environmentally friendly production processes.

In conclusion, imports of technology, expertise, and equipment for renewable energy can play a crucial role in attracting foreign direct investment in renewable energy projects in the Caribbean, which can help finance renewable energy development and promote economic growth. However, it is important that trade and investment policies are well-designed and implemented to promote environmentally friendly technologies and products and focus on the environmental performance of imported goods and services to mitigate the negative impacts of imports on the environment.

SUMMARY AND KEY FINDINGS

An analysis of importing goods for the public interest in the Caribbean utilizing faith-based organizations and government partnerships has found the following key findings:

Faith-based organizations and government partnerships can be essential in promoting renewable energy development and reducing dependence on fossil fuels in the Caribbean.

These partnerships can help overcome the challenges of limited resources and infrastructure by pooling resources and working together.

They can also help to attract foreign investment in renewable energy projects, create jobs, and boost economic growth.

These partnerships can also help improve access to electricity in rural and remote areas, a challenge in many Caribbean countries.

Faith-based organizations and government partnerships can also promote sustainable development and mitigate the negative impacts of imports on the environment.

These partnerships raise awareness and promote public engagement in addressing energy and environmental challenges in the Caribbean.

Through these partnerships, Caribbean countries can share knowledge and resources and collaborate to develop renewable energy projects and reduce dependence on fossil fuels.

It is essential that these partnerships are well-designed and implemented and consider the economic, social, and environmental factors.

In summary, partnerships between faith-based organizations and the government can effectively promote renewable energy development and reduce dependence on fossil fuels in the Caribbean. These partnerships can help overcome the challenges of limited resources and infrastructure, attract foreign investment, create jobs, and boost economic growth, improve access to electricity in rural and remote areas and promote sustainable development.

JAMAICA'S POTENTIAL ROLE IN IMPORTING AND EXPORTING FOR CARIBBEAN ISLANDS

Jamaica's Potential Role in Importing and Exporting for Caribbean Islands. Jamaica has the potential to play a significant role in importing and exporting for Caribbean islands due to its location and infrastructure. As the largest trade port in Kingston and one of the largest faith-based institutions in the Caribbean, Jamaica is well-positioned to facilitate trade and distribution throughout the region.

The Port of Kingston, Jamaica, is the main port of entry and exit for goods in Jamaica and plays a crucial role in the country's economy. As one of the Caribbean's largest ports, it can handle a significant volume of trade and is a hub for the movement of goods throughout the region. The port has undergone considerable modernization and expansion in recent years, including constructing a new container terminal and improving efficiency and capacity.

Additionally, Jamaica has a strong network of faith-based organizations that could significantly distribute imported goods to remote and underserved areas. These organizations have a strong presence in communities and have residents' trust. Utilizing these organizations as distribution points could increase access to goods and services in these areas and promote economic development.

Jamaica's location also plays a crucial role in its potential as an import and export hub. The country is strategically located in the Caribbean, making it easily accessible to other Caribbean islands, Central and South America, and North America. This proximity could enable Jamaica to serve as a gateway for trade between these regions, facilitating the import and export of goods and services.

However, Jamaica also faces challenges that could limit its potential as an import and export hub. The country has a high debt-to-GDP ratio, which could make it challenging to finance large-scale infrastructure projects. Additionally,

Jamaica has a relatively small domestic market, which could limit the potential for growth in domestic consumption.

In conclusion, Jamaica has the potential to play a significant role in importing and exporting for Caribbean islands due to its location, infrastructure, and the presence of faith-based organizations. However, the country also faces some challenges that could limit its potential. To fully take advantage of these opportunities, Jamaica must address its economic challenges and continue investing in infrastructure and trade-related activities.

RECOMMENDATIONS FOR FUTURE ACTION

There are several recommendations for future action that can be taken to promote and facilitate imports for the public good in Caribbean islands:

1. 1. Utilize faith-based organizations as distribution points: Utilizing faith-based organizations as distribution points for imported goods can increase access to goods and services in remote and underserved areas and promote economic development.

2. 2. Improve transportation and communication infrastructure: Improving transportation and communication infrastructure can facilitate importing and exporting of goods and services and promote economic development.

3. 3. Promote digital inclusion: Promoting digital inclusion and access to technology can help to develop small businesses and increase access to government services in Caribbean islands

4. 4. Invest in trade-related activities: Investing in trade- related activities such as improving ports, trade facilitation, and other trade-related infrastructure can help to increase trade and economic growth in the Caribbean islands.

5. 5. Address economic challenges: Addressing economic challenges such as high debt-to-GDP ratio and small domestic market can help to make Caribbean islands more attractive to trade and investment

6. 6. Jamaica should take advantage of its location and infrastructure to become an import and export hub for the Caribbean islands.

7. 7. Jamaica should continue to invest in the modernization and expansion of the Port of Kingston to improve efficiency and capacity.

8. 8. Jamaica should explore opportunities for trade with other Caribbean islands, Central and South America, and North America to facilitate the import and export of goods and services.

9. 9. Jamaica should consider providing trade licenses for foreign companies to operate within the country; this can increase trade volume and promote economic development.

10. 10. Jamaica should also consider developing regulations and policies that promote food security, public health, and safety.

11.

CONCLUSION AND FINAL THOUGHTS

In conclusion, integrating public, private, and faith-based organizations for importing and exporting goods is a promising approach for empowering the public in food security, education, housing, public safety, renewable energy, and technology innovation. This approach can create economic growth models for Caribbean governments and restore faith-based structures.

By partnering with private and faith-based organizations, governments can leverage their resources and expertise to improve the import and export of goods and services and promote economic development in Caribbean islands.

Additionally, by investing in infrastructure such as transportation and communication and promoting digital inclusion, governments can improve access to goods and services and help to develop small businesses.

Furthermore, by addressing economic challenges such as high debt-to-GDP ratio and small domestic market, Caribbean islands can become more attractive to trade and investment. With its location and infrastructure, Jamaica can play a vital role as an import and export hub for the Caribbean islands.

To achieve these goals, it is essential for Caribbean governments to work closely with private and faith-based organizations and to create policies and regulations that promote food security, public health, and safety.

Additionally, they should explore opportunities for trade with other Caribbean islands, Central and South America, and North America to facilitate the import and export of goods and services.

Integrating public, private, and faith-based organizations for importing and exporting goods can promote economic development, improve food security, and increase Caribbean island access to goods and services.

CARIBBEAN GOVERNMENT SOCIAL IMPACT MODELS

Model 1: Public-Private Partnership (PPP) Under this model, the government partners with a private company, such as a faith-based organization, to import goods to the public. The private company provides the necessary funding and resources to import the goods, while the government provides the regulatory framework and oversight. This model is beneficial as it allows the government to leverage the resources and expertise of the private sector while also ensuring that the imports comply with the country's laws and regulations.

Model 2: Community-Based Importation Under this model, faith-based organizations work with the community to import goods to the public. The community members are actively involved in the process, from identifying the goods needed to the actual importation process. This model is beneficial as it promotes community empowerment and engagement and gives the community a direct say in what goods are imported.

Model 3: Joint Venture Under this model, the government partners with a faith-based organization to form a joint venture to import goods to the public. The joint venture is a separate legal entity with its assets and liabilities. The government and the faith-based organization share the profits and losses of the experience. This model is beneficial as it allows the government and faith-based organization to pool their resources and expertise to import goods more efficiently and effectively.

Model 4: Grant-Based Importation Under this model, the government grants faith-based organizations the to import goods to the public. Faith-based organizations use grants to cover the costs of importing the goods and delivering them to the community. This model is beneficial as it allows the government to provide targeted assistance to faith-based organizations that are working on importing goods to the public while also ensuring that the imports comply with the country's laws and regulations.

FAITH-BASED IMPORT MODELS

1. **Public-Private Partnership Model:** The government partners with faith-based organizations to import goods that will benefit the public. The government provides financial support and resources, while faith-based organizations use their networks and expertise to import and distribute goods to those in need.

2. **Community-Based Distribution Model:** Faith- based organizations import goods and distribute them to their local communities. The organizations work closely with community leaders and members to identify specific needs and ensure that the goods are distributed fairly and efficiently.

3. **Social Enterprise Model:** In this model, faith- based organizations import goods and sell them fairly to the public. The profits from the sales are then used to fund social programs and initiatives that benefit the community. This model helps to create a sustainable source of funding for the organization and provides much-needed goods to the community.

4. **Micro-Finance Model:** In this model, faith-based organizations import goods and provide microfinance loans to small business owners and entrepreneurs in the community. The loans are used to purchase the goods, which are then sold to the public. This model helps to create jobs and economic opportunities in the community.

5. **Volunteer-Based Model:** Faith-based organizations import goods and rely on volunteers to help distribute them to the community. This model is beneficial in times of crisis or the mobilization of faith-based volunteers to provide aid and assistance.

LEARNING ASSESSMENT

Objective: To evaluate the reader's understanding and comprehension of the material covered in the book "Empowering the Caribbean Islands: The Role of Imports for Social Impact."

Instructions:

1. Read through each question carefully and select the best answer.

2. Once you have completed all questions, check your answers and see how you scored.

Question 1: What is the main focus of the book?

a. The history of Caribbean imports

b. The economic growth of Caribbean countries

c. The role of imports in empowering Caribbean islands for social impact

d. The impact of faith-based organizations on Caribbean imports

Question 2: Which organizations are discussed in the book as key players in the importing and exporting process in the Caribbean?

a. Public organizations only

b. Private organizations only

c. Faith-based organizations only

d. Public, private and faith-based organizations

Question 3: How does the author suggest addressing the challenges faced by Caribbean island nations regarding food security, education, housing, public safety, renewable energy, and technological innovation?

a. By increasing government spending

b. By decreasing government regulations

c. By integrating public, private, and faith-based organizations

d. By increasing tourism

Question 4: What is the main benefit of importing goods for the Caribbean islands, according to the author?

a. It creates jobs

b. It improves the economy

c. It empowers the people for social impact

d. It increases tourism

Question 5: What is the author's recommendation for future action for the Caribbean islands?

a. Increase government spending

b. Decrease government regulations

c. Integrate public, private, and faith-based organizations

d. Increase tourism

ANSWER KEY

1. c) The role of imports in empowering Caribbean islands for social impact

2. d) Public, private and faith-based organizations

3. c) By integrating public, private, and faith-based organizations

4. c) It empowers the people for social impact

5. c) Integrate public, private, and faith-based organizations

FAQ

Book Reviewer Question

1. What is Faith-based organizations' role in distributing imported goods to the public?

Author's Response

a. Partnering with private and public organizations to import goods that meet the community's needs.

b. Using their network and resources to distribute imported goods to those in need, such as through food banks, housing programs, and educational initiatives.

c. I am advocating for policies and programs that support the distribution of imported goods to the public, particularly those in need.

d. Providing education and training programs to help individuals and families become more self-sufficient and better equipped to access and utilize imported goods.

e. Build relationships and partnerships with other organizations and government agencies to better serve the community's needs.

The role of faith-based organizations in distributing imported goods to the public is to provide support, resources, and advocacy to improve the lives of those they serve.

Book Reviewer Question

2. How will faith-based organizations collect funds from the public to pay for goods?

Author's Response

Plan for Faith-Based Organization to Collect Money and Pay Importer/Small Business:

1. *Establish a system for collecting funds:* Faith-based organizations should create a method for collecting funds from their members and other contributors. This can be done through regular contributions, fundraising events, or online donations.

2. *Identify the goods and services to be imported:* Based on the community's needs, the faith-based organization should determine what goods and services they need to import. This could include food items, medical supplies, construction materials, or technology products.

3. *Contact importers and small businesses:* The faith-based organization should reach out to them to determine the cost of importing the goods and services they need.

4. *Create a budget:* Based on the cost of importing the goods and services, the faith-based organization should create a budget for collecting funds and paying the importer/small business.

5. *Set up a payment system:* The faith-based organization should establish a payment system for paying the importer/small business. This can be done through a check, wire transfer, or online payment platform.

6. *Monitor and evaluate the process: The faith-based organization should monitor and evaluate the process of collecting funds and paying the importer/small business. This will help them identify any challenges or opportunities for improvement and make adjustments as needed.*

7. *Celebrate successes: When the process is successful, and the goods and services have been imported and distributed to the community, the faith-based organization should celebrate its successes and express gratitude to its members, contributors, and the importer/small business.*

By following this plan, faith-based organizations can effectively collect funds, import goods and services, and distribute them to the public while supporting small businesses and importers in their communities.

Book Reviewer Question

3. Does your Faith-Based organization distribution model change the "Role of Faith-Based Organization"?

Author's Response

1. *Historically, churches have been crucial in serving as distribution centers for goods in various communities. This practice can be traced back to the early Christian communities, where the church served as a hub for social and economic activities, including the distribution of goods.*

2. *In medieval Europe, churches were often at the center of towns and villages, providing essential services such as education, healthcare, and food distribution to the local community. During times of crisis or disaster, churches would often step up to distribute supplies and aid to those in need.*

3. *In the modern era, faith-based organizations, including churches, continue to serve as important centers for community service and support. They often provide food pantries, clothing drives, and other aid programs to those in need. In many developing countries, faith- based organizations are often the primary source of support for marginalized communities, providing education, healthcare, and economic support.*

4. *The role of faith-based organizations in distributing goods to the public is broader than just providing aid and support during times of crisis. Many faith-based organizations also operate thrift stores, food banks, and other initiatives to provide ongoing support to their communities. These organizations often partner with local businesses and importers to bring essential goods, such as food, clothing, and household items, and distribute them to those in need.*

5. *In conclusion, the historical precedent for faith-based organizations serving as distribution centers for goods is strong, and these organizations continue to play a critical role in supporting communities worldwide.*

6. *Whether providing aid during times of crisis, operating thrift stores and food banks, or partnering with local businesses and importers to bring in essential goods, faith-based organizations are an important part of the fabric of many communities.*

Book Reviewer Question

4. How can Caribbean countries become an exporter of renewable energy and its components?

Author's Response

There are several ways that Caribbean countries can become exporters of renewable energy and its components. Some of these include:

A. **Investment in renewable energy:** *Caribbean countries can invest in renewable energy sources like solar, wind, and hydropower. This can include the installation of new infrastructure and the development of new technologies.*

B. **Promoting renewable energy:** *Caribbean countries can promote renewable energy through tax incentives, subsidies, and other financial incentives. This can increase demand for renewable energy and create new business opportunities for exporters.*

C. **Collaboration with other countries:** *Caribbean countries can collaborate to share knowledge and expertise in renewable energy. This can help accelerate the development of new technologies and increase the competitiveness of Caribbean exporters in the global market.*

D. **Development of local renewable energy companies:** *Caribbean countries can encourage the development of local renewable energy companies. This can help create jobs and improve the competitiveness of local companies in the global market.*

E. **Diversification of energy sources:** *Caribbean countries can diversify their energy sources by promoting using multiple renewable energy sources. This can help reduce dependence on a single energy source and increase the energy system's resilience.*

Overall, the key to becoming an exporter of renewable energy and its components is to create a supportive environment for the development and growth of renewable energy industries. Can be accomplished by investing in infrastructure, promoting the use of renewable energy, collaborating with other countries, and supporting local companies.

Book Reviewer Question

5. How will your plan drive Caribbean government involvement, and What policies will be needed?

Author's Response

To drive Caribbean government involvement in the export of renewable energy and its components, a comprehensive plan that outlines the benefits and opportunities for the country and its people should be developed. This plan should clearly articulate the vision and goals for the renewable energy sector and the steps necessary to achieve them.

The following policies will be needed to support the development of the renewable energy sector in the Caribbean:

A. *Regulatory framework*: A clear and supportive regulatory framework is necessary to provide stability and certainty required for investors, developers, and manufacturers to invest in the renewable energy sector. This should include incentives for renewable energy generation, such as tax credits, subsidies, and feed-in tariffs.

B. *Infrastructure development*: The Caribbean countries must invest in infrastructure development to support the growth of renewable energy. This includes the development of transmission and distribution networks, as well as the construction of renewable energy power plants.

C. *Skills and capacity building*: The Caribbean governments must invest in developing the local workforce to ensure they have the skills and expertise to support the growth of the renewable energy sector. This includes training programs, education, and research and development initiatives.

D. Access to financing: The Caribbean governments must work with financial institutions and investors to provide access to funding for renewable energy projects. This will help to ensure that the renewable energy sector can grow and expand, providing jobs and economic opportunities for the people of the Caribbean.

E. International collaboration: The Caribbean governments must collaborate with other countries, regional organizations, and international institutions to share best practices, technology, and expertise in developing the renewable energy sector. This will help to ensure that the Caribbean is well-positioned to take advantage of the global shift towards renewable energy.

In conclusion, a comprehensive policy and regulatory framework, investment in infrastructure, skills and capacity building, access to financing, and international collaboration are all crucial elements for the successful development of the renewable energy sector in the Caribbean.

Book Reviewer Question

6. *How will your methods mentioned in this book drive digital infrastructure improvement and address the digital divide in the Caribbeans?*

Author's Response

The methods mentioned in this book can drive digital infrastructure improvement and address the digital divide in the Caribbean by promoting the adoption of digital technologies in importing and distributing goods by faith-based organizations. By leveraging technology, these organizations can increase efficiency, reach more people, and provide more opportunities for remote and underserved communities. Additionally, by promoting digital skills training and providing access to digital tools and devices, faith-based organizations can help to bridge the digital divide and create a more inclusive and connected Caribbean.

The book can highlight the benefits of digital technologies for import and distribution and faith-based organizations' role in promoting these technologies. Governments can be encouraged to implement policies that support digital infrastructure development, increase access to technology and digital tools, and provide training and support for organizations and individuals to use these tools effectively. By promoting the adoption of digital technologies and driving government involvement, the book can help to create a more connected, inclusive, and sustainable Caribbean that is better equipped to meet the needs of its citizens and compete in a global market.

Book Reviewer Question

7. How will Caribbean countries export pure energy to adjoining islands?

Author's Response

Exporting pure energy to adjoining islands, Caribbean countries would need to implement several steps, including the following:

1. *Assessment of energy resources: Conduct a comprehensive evaluation of the energy resources available in the country, including renewable energy sources such as wind, solar, and hydropower.*

2. *Development of energy infrastructure: Develop energy infrastructure, including power plants and distribution networks, to harness and transmit energy from renewable sources.*

3. *Investment in technology: Invest in technology and equipment needed for energy production, such as wind turbines, solar panels, and hydroelectric systems.*

4. *Interconnections with neighboring islands: Establish interconnections to transmit energy and allow energy flow between countries.*

5. *Government policies: Develop government policies and regulations to support the growth and development of the renewable energy sector, such as tax incentives and grants.*

6. *Partnerships with the private sector: Foster partnerships with the private sector, including energy companies, to spur investment in renewable energy projects and provide technical expertise.*

7. *Regional cooperation: Promote regional cooperation among Caribbean countries to ensure a harmonized approach to renewable energy development and export.*

By implementing these steps, Caribbean countries can become significant exporters of renewable energy and its components to adjoining islands, helping to promote sustainable development and reduce dependence on fossil fuels.

Book Reviewer Question

8. What is the mile radius for adjourning pure renewable energy with the sources suggested in this book?

Author's Response

The mile radius for exporting renewable energy to adjoining islands will depend on several factors, such as the type of renewable energy source, the infrastructure available, the source's location, and the target island's location. For example, wind energy can be exported over longer distances than solar energy. The transmission technology and grid connectivity will also play a role in determining the length over which can be exported.

Considering these factors and conducting a comprehensive analysis to determine the appropriate mile radius for exporting renewable energy to adjoining islands is important.

The type of transmission technology and grid connectivity required to connect energy sources between Caribbean islands will depend on several factors, including the distance between islands, the amount of energy to be transmitted, and the specific type of renewable energy being used.

For short-distance transmission, direct high-voltage current (HVDC) technology is more efficient for transmitting large amounts of power over long distances. For longer distances, alternating current (AC) technology may be required, as HVDC cables are more expensive and difficult to install over longer distances.

A robust and reliable interconnectivity system between islands is crucial in terms of grid connectivity. This will allow for a seamless flow of energy between islands, which will help to improve energy security and reliability. To achieve this, it may be necessary to install high-voltage submarine cables, which will connect the grids of different islands and allow for energy exchange between them.

It's also important to note that interconnecting the grids of different Caribbean islands will require close coordination and cooperation between the governments and relevant stakeholders in each island, as well as investments in the necessary infrastructure and technology.